THE BESTWORDS

- POSTS OF MAD COMEDIANS -

THE BEST WORDS

- POSTS OF MAD COMEDIANS -

Conceived & Edited By
Carol Siskind

Art Direction By
Bob Johnson & Carol Siskind

Design & Layout By Bob Johnson
BittenByAZebra.com

I dedicate this effort to the memory of my parents,
Teri & Bill Siskind, who taught me the meaning of empathy,

Carol Siskind
October 2018

•••

This book is made possible by the following individuals, who have donated their time and talent to this cause. Much appreciation to:

KEVIN ROONEY, for your support, encouragement, and "The Best Words."

PAT BUCKLES, for making the impossible possible.

MAUREEN LANGAN, for your proofreading expertise.

BOB JOHNSON, for your brilliant layout and design skills which have brought my vision to fruition; for the countess hours you've devoted to this project, and for graciously accommodating more than my 'two cents.' I love you.

And of course, to my fellow comedians, for your exceptional contributions:

Tamer Kattan
John DeBellis
Neal Brennan **Glenn Hirsch**
Maureen Langan
Sarah Silverman
Charles Zucker
Jason Stuart **Leah Krinsky**
Jann Karam **Kevin Rooney**
Mark Brazill **Bill McCarty**
Kevin Nealon
Rudy Reber **Mike Rowe**
Erin O'Connor
Rob Becker **Rick Overton** **Eileen Conn**
Diane Nichols **Dana Gould**
Merrill Markoe
Mike Dugan **Carl Reiner** **Dennis Blair**
Stephen Tupper
William Stephenson
Jonathan Schmock
Wendy Liebman
Larry Amoros
Cathy Ladman
Gabe Abelson

October 2018

"The Best Words: Posts of Mad Comedians" was born from the shared disgust I and my fellow comedians have for the current administration's callousness and cruelty, which only serve to destroy our spirit and gut our democracy. Their heartless policy of ripping children from their parents' arms was the last straw for me.

While I applaud the journalists and politicians speaking truth to power, it's my colleagues in the comedy community whose angry, humorous, pithy social media posts I turn to daily to reassure me that I am not alone. And so, the decision to harness their posts for the greater good was made.

All net proceeds from this book will go towards reuniting and helping families who come to our beloved country seeking asylum.

The posts start just before the inauguration of 2017 and go to date of publication.

Let our unique community shine a light during these dark times.

With heartfelt gratitude,

Carol

Kevin Rooney
January 7, 2018

•••

"I have the best words, but I don't have the words to describe the words I have."

— Stable Genius "Failing" Donald Trump

Mike Rowe
December 31, 2016

Midnight, Times Square: we'll be reminded that America dropped the ball.

Mike Rowe
December 24, 2016

The Trump inaugural is down to one Rockette.

Erin O'Connor
January 12, 2017

I don't hate Donald Trump; he's just not my cup of pee.

Kevin Rooney
January 19, 2017

I feel, as I brace for Trump's swearing-in tomorrow, like a father about to walk his beloved, only daughter down the aisle into the arms of a known felon and mobster who has promised me he has reformed himself and will dedicate himself from now on to his new career as the money-shot specialist in porn films.

John DeBellis
2016 • Twitter

• • •

Trump's doctor released more extensive medical records. This time they were hand written on an entire pack of rolling papers.

Kevin Rooney
January 20, 2017

• • •

Most heard comment on news programs today: "Meanwhile Washington prepares for the peaceful perversion of power."

Bill McCarty
2016

• • •

Circular Haiku

He rode in on fear:
Orange tint, thin skin, weird hair.
Fuck him and the horse.

Kevin Rooney
January 6, 2018 at 1:28 PM

• • •

Hey Blotus, "The whole world is retching! The whole world is retching!..."

Kevin Rooney
January 7, 2018 at 1:28 PM

The blimperor has no clue!

Rick Overton
2017

The scariest part? His hair is real but combed to look fake.

Kevin Rooney
January 11, 2017 at 1:28 PM

Hey, Donnie! Urine trouble, pal!

Mike Rowe
December 29, 2016

Trump plans on an inaugural speech focused on 'unity,' and his hatred of Mexicans.

Erin O'Connor
January 10, 2017

Remind Inaugural Caterer: "No asparagus."

— Kellyanne Conway To Do List 01/10/17

Jann Karam
January 20, 2017

It's raining in D.C. Shouldn't he be melting soon?

Erin O'Connor
January 10, 2017

Trump told Japanese P.M. Abe that the White House is "very famous."

That's what you say when you take your guests to Jerry's Deli.

Jann Karam
January 20, 2017 • Women's March

Carol Siskind
January 20, 2017 • Women's March

Leah Krinsky
Women's March

Pussy is the new black.

Dana Gould
January 26, 2017

I'm a little concerned that the first move of the Trump administration is to redefine what "the truth" is.

Carol Siskind
January 20, 2017 • Women's March

Mike Dugan
January 2017

Hey, far-right, if you want the Congress you elected to stay away from your guns, make sure you don't keep them in your vagina.

Mike Dugan
January 2017

Guns don't kill people. People kill people. Corporations are people. Gun manufacturers are corporations. Gun manufacturers kill people.

Leah Krinsky
January 27, 2017 • Twitter

Trump doesn't mention Jews in today's Holocaust remarks because that would ruin the surprise.

John DeBellis
January 28, 2017 • Twitter

Trump had a phone conversation with Putin. I heard that Trump's very first words to Putin were, "What are you wearing?"

John DeBellis
Februay 2, 2017 • Twitter

Trump says he can't show you his taxes now because he's getting audited by the Russians.

John DeBellis
January 28, 2017 • Twitter

Congress is repealing the law that keeps guns away from the mentally ill in order to justify Trump having the nuclear codes.

"The Plan"

Jonathan Schmock

Carol Siskind
2017

It's ironic that this bloated, gluttonous vessel of a man is so empty.

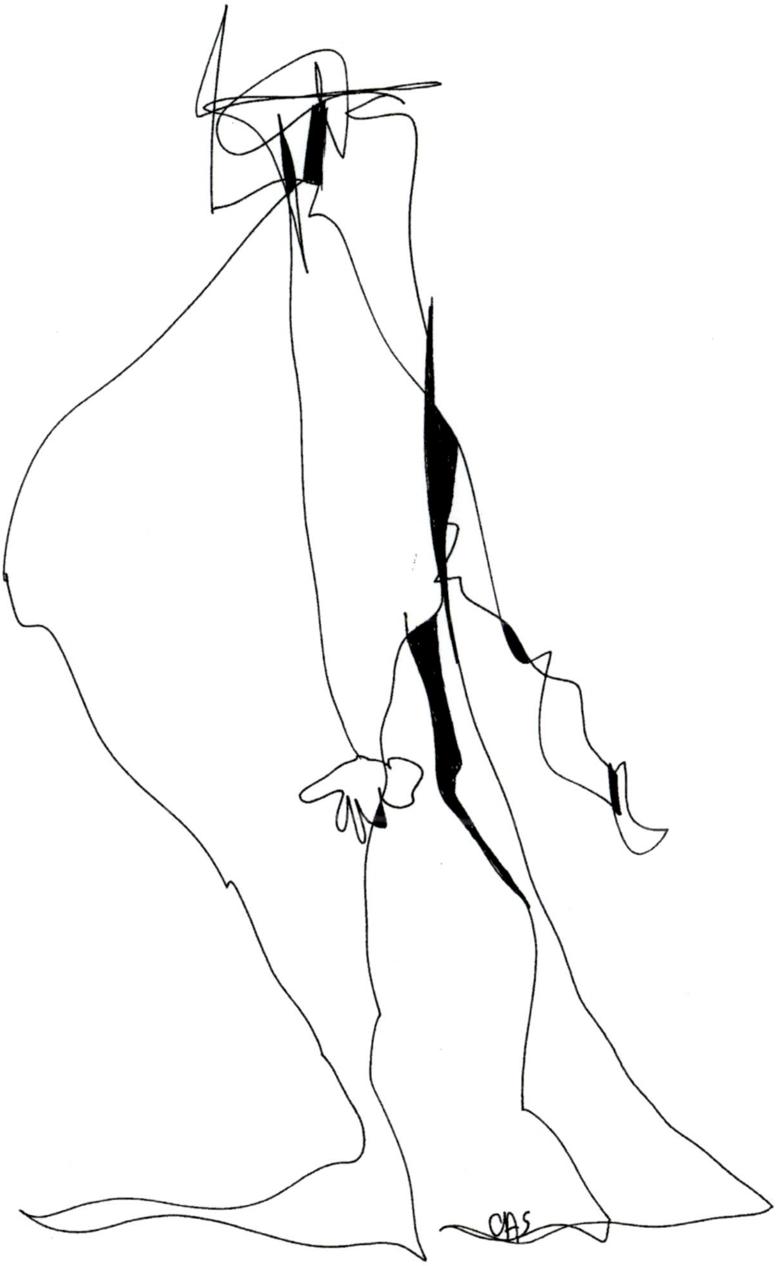

Eileen Conn
March 6, 2018

Happy Women's History Month, assholes!

Mike Rowe
March 6, 2017

New Trump ban poised to deport classic rock supergroup Foreigner.

Mike Rowe
March 17, 2017

Trump and his meeting with Merkel. He said, "It was difficult, she's not even a 3."

Leah Krinsky
March 29, 2017 • Twitter

I bet the Republicans who say they're against regulation of any kind all have a dominatrix telling them when they can pee.

•••

Jann Karam
March 29, 2017

•••

With the Drumpf admin, I no longer need an alarm clock to wake me up in the morning. Everyday, at the crack of dawn, I'm roused from my restless slumber by the sound of my own internal PANIC.

Gabe Abelson
March 29, 2017

•••

Ivanka Trump will take an unofficial, unpaid role in the Trump White House. You know, just like Putin.

Kevin Rooney
April 8, 2018

•••

Trump stumbles into a little personal truth when he says, "We have a problem with 'gina."

Jonathan Schmock

John DeBellis
May 7, 2017 • Twitter

I'm a fan of #JeffSessions.

I loved the way he played the banjo in *Deliverance*.

Mike Dugan
May 13, 2017

Listening to Trump talk about God feels like watching Richard Simmons explain the NFL draft.

Kevin Rooney
May 26, 2017

Trump uses the English language like a blind man uses a camera.

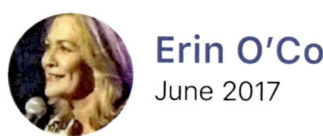

Erin O'Connor
June 2017

I like my covfefe like I like my presidents.

WE DON'T HAVE A PRESIDENT

WE HAVE A MASCOT

Jonathan Schmock

Wendy Liebman
2017

I've been worried about Russia and North Korea, and that I bought too many forever stamps.

Glenn Hirsch
July 20, 2017

Does character really matter? Or is it just about money? Asking for a friend.

Diane Nichols
May 24, 2017

They're creepy and they're kooky
Mysterious and spooky
They're all together ooky
The POTUS Family

Mike Rowe
June 2, 2017

Trump plans on a trip to Manila to thank them for the envelopes.

Leah Krinsky
June 12, 2017

I find it easier to shit a perfect replica of Michelangelo's David than to feel sorry for Ivanka Trump.

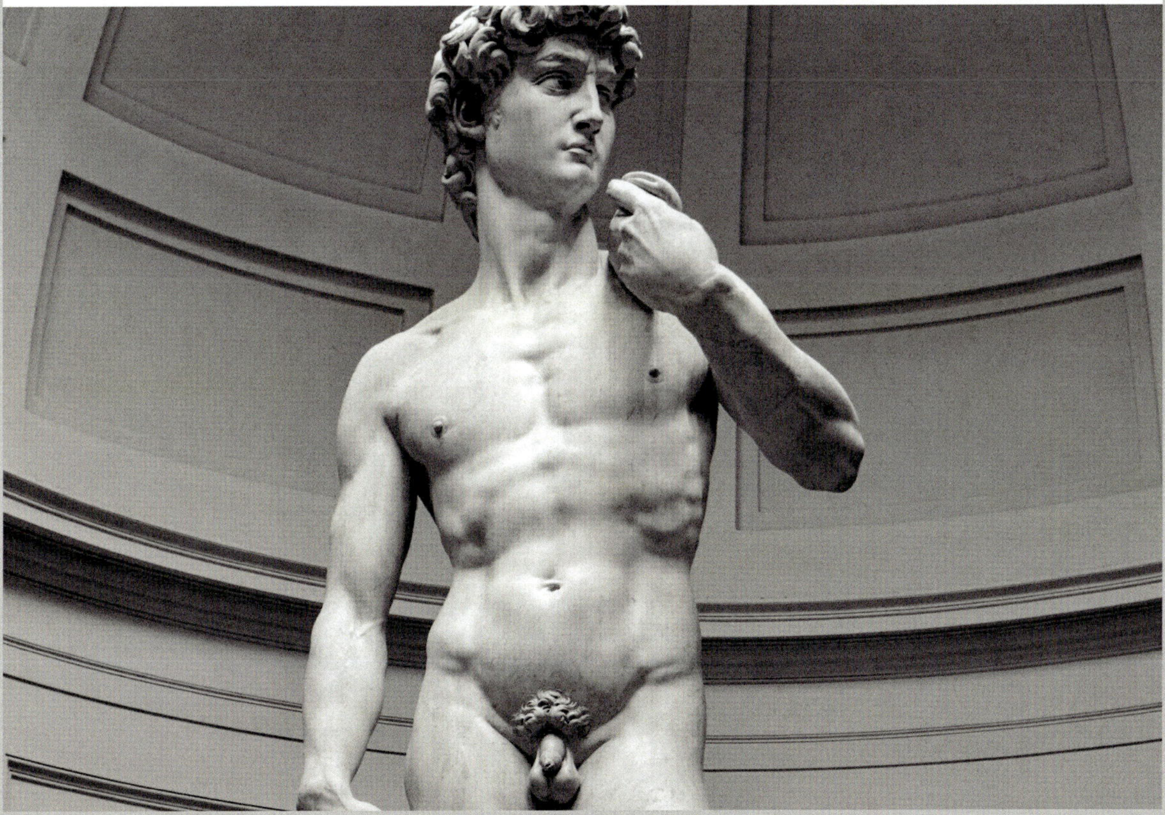

Mike Rowe
June 2, 2017

After Trump hugged the flag today, it made an official #metoo claim.

Bill McCarty
July 24, 2017

The illiterate gasbag in the White House doesn't even realize that when writing "Hillarys crimes," "Hillary's" requires an apostrophe. I can tolerate the fascism; it's the disdain for proper punctuation that drives me nuts.

Sarah Silverman
2017

No matter how different we are, we have to take care of each other.

Happy birthday, America. We're rooting for you.

Kevin Rooney
June 24, 2018

"I, Donald J. Trump, solemnly swear to execute the office of president of the United States." Obviously, he mistook the meaning of "execute."

Mike Dugan
July 7, 2017

I don't know if there's anything to the dementia rumors, but when Angela Merkel mentioned "G20" today, Trump yelled, "Bingo!"

Kevin Rooney
July 20, 2017 at 1:28 PM

The countdown has begun to Trump inviting O.J. to Mar-a-Lago for the Scumbags of America Pro-Am Golf Tournament.

Mike Dugan
July 21, 2017

Sean Spicer says he quit "to spend more time without Trump's family."

Mike Dugan
July 25, 2017

"I was never a Boy Scout, but I have no trouble pitching a tent, believe me. No problems in that area."

— Donald Trump addressing the Girl Scouts

Gabe Abelson
July 28, 2017

Know those movie previews that start out with the voice-over: "In a world gone mad...?"

This is it.

Carol Siskind
2017

That creepy okay sign is not working. Things are anything but okay.

Mike Dugan
August 18, 2017 at 10:24 AM

Verified by White House sources: "Gorka" is an actual sound you hear when Trump yanks an idea out of his ass.

•••

Dana Gould
2017

Apparently Trump's "office" doubles as the concierge desk at the Mar-a-Lago resort.

•••

Kevin Rooney
August 17, 2017

General Kelly listening to Trump on Tuesday looked like Preston Sturges getting script notes from Adam Sandler.

•••

Leah Krinsky
September 19, 2017

People are reading too much into these pics of John Kelly listening to Trump. Maybe Kelly just has Resting-Holy-Fuck-Shit-What-A-Goddamn-Imbecile-What-The-Hell-Was-I-Thinking-How-The-Fuck-Do-I-Get-Myself-Out-Of-This-Goddamn-Fucking-Shitshow-Sweet-Suffering-Jesus-Help-Me Face.

•••

"John Kelly & friend"

Jonathan Schmock

Kevin Rooney
August 18, 2017

Bannon's real offense to Trump? Stealing the slimelight.

Mike Dugan
September 26, 2017 at 10:24 AM

Trump should consider getting some rest. He's been burning the cross at both ends.

"Into the Darkness"
Jonathan Schmock

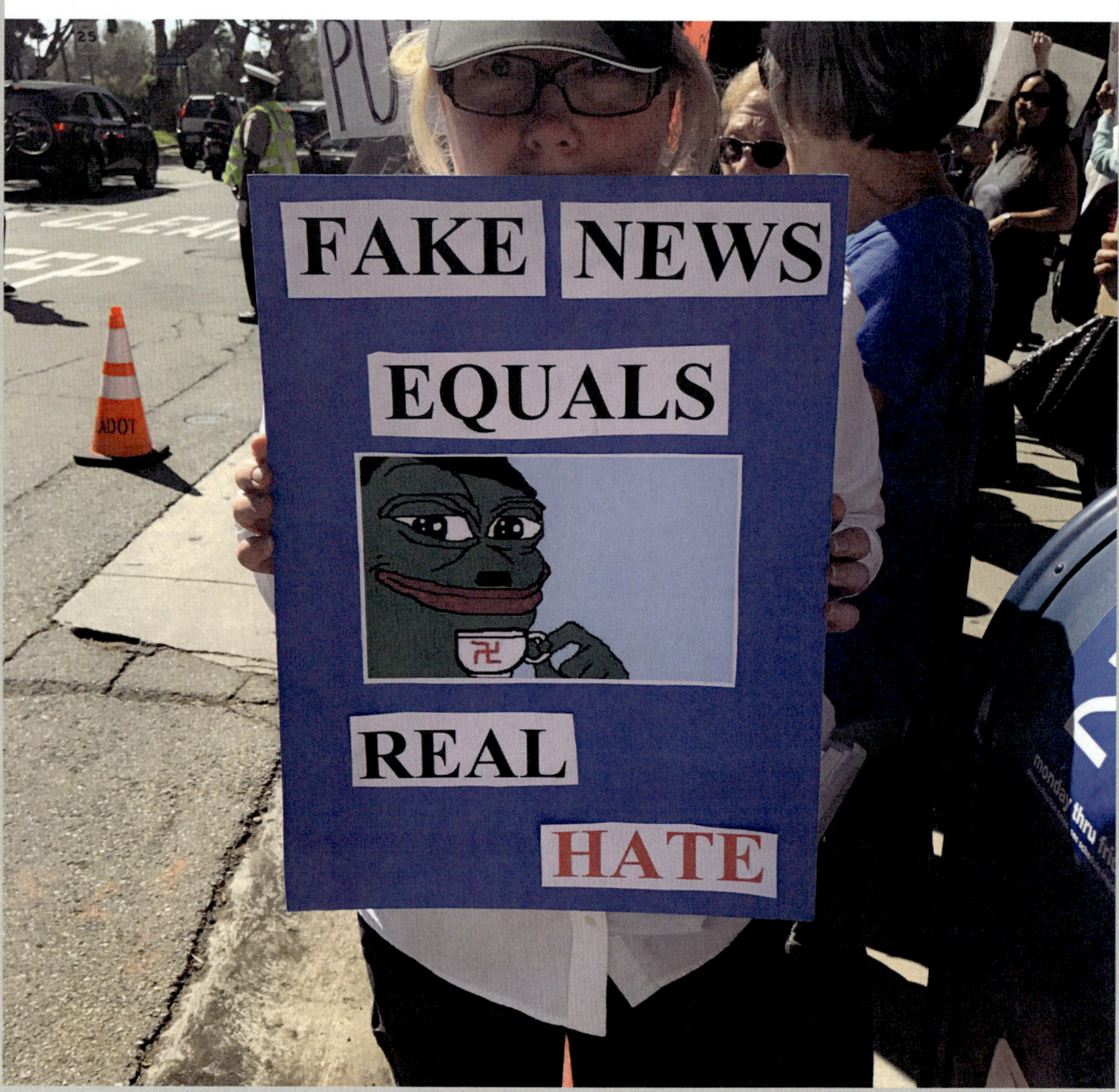

John DeBellis
2017 • Twitter

One thing I can say about Trump is that he'll never allow doing the right thing to cloud his judgment.

Jason Stuart
2017

Roy Cohn, the ruthless, closeted, gay lawyer was Trump's mentor. So does that mean he likes gays as long as they are lawyers?

Kevin Rooney
February 7, 2018

Trump has ordered new rubber stamps for the government, one-inch block letters in red: "Ineffective Immediately."

Leah Krinsky
March 13, 2017 • Twitter

If Obama did use microwaves to spy on Trump, he could face up to 45 seconds. #microwavegate

Carol Siskind
2017

Does this administration make me look fat? It should. I'm stuffing my face to muffle my screams.

Jann Karam
October 3, 2017 • Twitter

My family & I are moving to the #MiddleEast just to get away from the gun violence. #BanAssaultWeapons #StopTheViolence #2ndAmendment #warzone!

•••

Leah Krinsky
2017

•••

Can they put out an Amber Alert for the entire country? #MAGA

Charles Zucker
October 9, 2017

•••

Who said it?

"It's a shame the White House has become an adult day care center."

    A. Jimmy Fallon
    B. Jimmy Kimmel
    C. Trevor Noah

The answer is D. Republican Senator Bob Corker.

Eileen Conn
September 17, 2017

Fuck you, Emmys. You invited Spicer into our community? Fuck you. You normalized him. Fuck you.

Mike Rowe
February 25, 2017

Not looking forward to seeing America in the "In Memoriam" reel at the Oscars.

Mike Dugan
September 26, 2017

Trump hasn't dealt with the hurricane devastation in San Juan yet because every time someone says "RICO," he hides under his desk.

Mike Dugan
September 26, 2017

Until this morning Trump thought San Juan was one of his gardeners.

Bill McCarty
October 12, 2017

Trump, America's slumlord, is treating Puerto Rico like a property he has decided to torch for the insurance money. We all knew that people would die as a result of Trump becoming POTUS, and he is proving us right on a daily basis.

Larry Amoros
December 22, 2017

How can Mike Pence be homophobic when he spends so much time up Donald Trump's ass?

Leah Krinsky
December 19, 2017 • Twitter

Congrats, GOP tax bill – for getting through the House without anyone spotting the provision that allows the poor to be burned for fuel.

 **Mark Brazill**
2017

I want Trump to succeed when it comes to failing.

 **John DeBellis**
August 26, 2016 • Twitter

If Donald Trump spoke in the forest and no one was there to hear it, would he still sound like an idiot?

 **Neal Brennan**
December 22, 2017

Trump wouldn't be President if we'd have spelling bees instead of debates.

Carol Siskind
2017

His Official White House Portrait

Carol Siskind
2017

Her Official White House Portrait

Sarah Silverman
July 2, 2018

BE BEST.

Diane Nichols
June 21, 2018

The only comic relief we get is watching how much his wife has grown to hate him.

Leah Krinsky
March 6, 2018 • Twitter

Trump reversed ban on imports from trophy hunting. Wife #4: you've been warned.

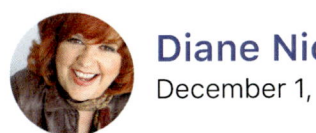

Diane Nichols
December 1, 2016

I would rather be forced to coach Melania Trump doing five minutes of standup at The Laugh Factory than ever hear Kellyanne Conway speak again.

Tamer Kattan
February 9, 2018 at 4:11 PM

I'm not gonna call Trump stupid, but I will say he seems like the kind of guy that pets cats too hard.

Rob Becker
January 12, 2018 at 2:08 PM

The Trump presidency feels like being trapped with a drunk driver in a '73 Pinto stuck in reverse.

Maureen Langan
2018

Trump caught with a porn star? I'd be more shocked if he were caught with a book.

Charles Zucker
October 23, 2017

Trump to release JFK docs and the tin foil hat industry rejoices.

Kevin Rooney
October 18, 2017

Trump the multi-tasker: lying, stealing, and sowing hate all at once.

Rick Overton
2017

This too shall pass, like a pinecone sized kidney stone. But it will pass.

Mike Rowe
March 17, 2017

Trump claims Don Jr. was his son for just a short time.

Leah Krinsky
November 27, 2017 • Twitter

Trump is regressing like the guy in "Flowers for Algernon," except Trump never had that brief time where he got to be smart.

Leah Krinsky
January 4, 2018 • Twitter

Trump supporters outraged over new Trump book and also over books in general.

Maureen Langan
2018

People say Trump doesn't read. Not true. He loves the classics: "Lord of the Lies," "Nasty Little Women," "Catch Her in the Pussy" and "The Joy of Sex (Especially When Your Lawyer Pays For It)."

This
Little Golden Shower Book
belongs to
Donald

NASTY LITTLE WOMEN

Cover Art: François Boucher - *La Toilette intime (Une Femme qui pisse)*, 1760s

Kevin Rooney
January 9, 2018

Republicans have their heads buried in Trump's ass – because it is the only way to get a face-to-face meeting with him.

Kevin Rooney
January 31, 2018

That big orange moon last night was God hanging Trump in effigy.

Kevin Rooney
April 21, 2018

A lot of the folks at Barbara Bush's funeral look like they could stay after her funeral – for their own.

Cathy Ladman
April 24, 2018 • Twitter

If Melania had fun with the Obamas at Barbara Bush's funeral, imagine how much fun she'll have with them at Trump's funeral.

Dana Gould
June 24, 2018

It's very hard to find a photo of Melania Trump looking genuinely happy – unless she's in the company of someone her husband hates. Then she lights right up!

Leah Krinsky
February 4, 2018 • Twitter

The only reason Hope Hicks has a job at the White House is in case they need spare parts for Melania.

Maureen Langan
2018

Melania speaks five languages and she hates her husband in all of them, including body language.

Kevin Rooney
January 22, 2018

See, it's no different than it has always been: We the People of the United States, in Order to form a more perfect Union, will throw out all the different-looking people and keep them out. "All for wan, wan for all."

Kevin Rooney
January 29, 2018

Trump does not need to say a word about the state of the Union. Just looking at him will tell us all we need to know: the Union is bloated, vain, sick and stupid. The Union is shifty, guilt-ridden and criminal. The Union is in big trouble.

Mike Dugan
January 2018

I just watched the Eric Trump interview on CNBC. Eric said "my father" more times in 13 minutes than Jesus did in 33 years.

"Cover Up"

Jonathan Schmock

Carol Siskind
2018

I'm hoping to lower my shoulders before 2020.

Carl Reiner
2018 • Twitter

If someone has stolen something, shouldn't the thief be forced to return his ill-gotten gains to its rightful owner (a.k.a. Hillary Clinton)?

Kevin Nealon
2018

Carol Siskind
2018

"Mourning: America's Pastime"

Maureen Langan
2018

"Over the rainbow" is a prepositional phrase. "Under the desk" is a school shooting.

Merrill Markoe
August 27, 2018

The U.S. is not only doing NOTHING about gun violence, it's also adjusting to mass shootings as a ho-hum part of daily life. So, I predict niche marketing to potential mass shooters: Half-Off Shooters Day Sale! Bullets! Note pads! Duct tape! Dictionary of ominous threats!

"**Armed Teachers**"

Jonathan Schmock

Glenn Hirsch
2018

There is talk of arming teachers in schools. If that had been the case in my day, I would've been dead by the third grade.

Leah Krinsky
February 25, 2018

Nobody should be forced to bake a wedding cake for someone who isn't marrying their gun.

Rob Becker
October 3, 2017

Remember who wants the shooters to have guns, and who doesn't want the victims to have health care.

Mark Brazill
2017

Law banning mental patients from owning a gun undone by Trump. Playin' to the base.

Dennis Blair
March 25, 2018

The guy who said he'd run into a shooting scene unarmed took the long way back from his golf club to avoid protesters.

#MarchForOurLives #COWARD

Mike Dugan
May 22, 2018

I'd like to pry your gun from your cold dead hands, but all of the cold dead hands I see aren't yours.

Tamer Kattan
February 9, 2018 at 4:11 PM

Today's shooting happened in Texas, America's most gun-friendly state, and it happened with armed security on the school campus. We don't need a wall when all the real monsters are living on our side of it.

Fuck the NRA and Fuck Trump.

Leah Krinsky
February 21, 2018

Yes, more guns in schools is precisely what we need to stop all the school shootings. Jesus fucking Christ, you idiot chunk of syphilitic baboon smegma.

Mike Dugan
February 21, 2018

Teachers with guns?? I'm still working through nuns with rulers.

Leah Krinsky
September 1, 2018 at 5:13 PM

September means pumpkin spice guns!

Leah Krinsky
June 16, 2018 • Twitter

2016 will be remembered as the year Bowie, Prince, and Democracy all died.

Bob Johnson
May 18, 2018

THOUGHTS & PRAYERS

Gabe Abelson
February 13, 2018

Trump said he doesn't understand why America celebrates Lincoln's birthday, adding, "I like presidents who weren't shot."

Kevin Rooney
July 25, 2018

Lincoln?! You're not as smart as a Lincoln log!

Mike Rowe
February 21, 2017

Trump claims he's a lot like Lincoln. I hope he's a big fan of the theater.

Neal Brennan
October 8, 2016 • Hootsuite

Right now, the Republican Party is a pussy being grabbed by Donald Trump. And they're letting him do it because he's a star.

Bill McCarty
March 18, 2017

The "madman theory" of diplomacy is so much more interesting when you use actual madmen.

Mike Dugan
May 13, 2018

Everything is fine here. The White House is running like Clockwork Orange.

Sarah Silverman
2018

It's not the people being lied to that I hate. They are just trusting and believing the lies that liars are saying. But I have NO TIME for liars, and liars live & work in the White House.

Carl Reiner
August 9, 2018 • Twitter

I commend Trump and his staff for the magnificent job they are doing to hasten our president's removal from office.

Mike Dugan
December 22, 2016

Kellyanne Conway is the "secretary of gaslighting."

Leah Krinsky
February 3, 2017

I consider Kellyanne Conway an object lesson in what happens when you choose to believe you're above needing either a moral compass or cosmetic injectables.

Diane Nichols
February 28, 2017

How about Kellyanne Conway being casually perched on the Oval Office couch, with her shoes on like a teenager, during an important photo shoot with leaders of Black universities? Anyone notice how far apart her knees are in the short dress? It looks like she went to a party in a VIP suite in Vegas and still isn't sober enough to leave in the morning.

Kellyanne

Carol Siskind
2018

As our beloved country gently weeps...

Mike Rowe
April 14, 2018

Trump asks 'Fox & Friends' to step down as White House advisors.

Mike Rowe
January 16, 2018

Trump clarifies that he hates racism and people of color.

Tamer Kattan
2018 • Twitter

Thank you @realDonaldTrump it is because of your level of hate and insensitivity that America has finally empathized with a Muslim family.

Sarah Silverman
2018

We're a nation of immigrants and a nation of hatred and a nation of love, but mostly we're a nation of people wanting to be loved.

Tamer Kattan
2018 • Twitter

America won't be great again by making it harder to be a citizen. It will be great if we make it harder for people like Trump to stay one.

Rob Becker
February 22, 2018

Trump always sounds like a cross between a sleazy salesman and a kid bluffing a report on a book he never read.

Mike Rowe
2018

I can't take Trump reading the teleprompter; it's like an 8th grader reading his book report about a book he never read.

Sarah Silverman
2018

I don't think it's right to make fun of dummies unless those dummies have immense power and are using their power for dumminess.

Mike Rowe
March 20, 2018

If Trump shot himself on 5th Avenue — his poll numbers would go up.

Mike Dugan
March 10, 2018

Trump just shot Stormy Daniels on 5th Avenue.

Leah Krinsky
April 14, 2018 • Twitter

If we have to have an arrogant, freakish, crazy old misogynist asshole with weird hair for president, why can't it at least be Karl Lagerfeld?

Carol Siskind
Women's March 2018

Kevin Rooney
January 5, 2017

For a guy who has not spent a single second in military service, Trump sure can execute an about-face.

Rob Becker
October 30, 2017

People who searched for corruption with a magnifying glass for eight years have suddenly developed glaucoma.

Tamer Kattan
April 13, 2018

Me: What are you thinking about, Garry?
Garry: Obama

Kevin Rooney
February 28, 2017

Trump and the GOP are not going to repeal Obamacare.
They are going to repeal and replace the people Obama
cared for.

Sarah Silverman
2017

Money is a drug. This country is being controlled and
destroyed by drug addicts.

Mike Dugan
April 15, 2018

Trump paid Stormy Daniels $130,000 in hush money. He paid $150,000 for Karen MacDougal's silence. The doorman at Trump Tower was paid $30,000 to shut up. Let history show that Trump's greatest presidential achievement was ending the gender pay gap.

Mike Dugan
March 23, 2018

To be fair, he also told Ruth Bader Ginsberg she reminds him of Ivanka.

Leah Krinsky
March 26, 2018 • Twitter

Once a guy I was having sex with told me I reminded him of his daughter (while I was choking him), so Stormy, I can totally relate.
#StormyDaniels

Mike Dugan
May 20, 2018

Stormy was his porn star. His Russian hookers were stormy, with occasional showers.

Kevin Rooney
July 24, 2018 at 10:22 PM

Trump: I didn't say "cash." I meant to say "gash," so the sentence should be, "Let's pay the gash," okay?

"Cuddling Among the Sheets"

Jonathan Schmock

Carol Siskind
2018

There isn't one neuron of my being that isn't frayed, frazzled, or fried.

"Burning the Constitution"

Jonathan Schmock

Sarah Silverman
June 10, 2018 • Twitter

It scrambles my brain that people clutch their 'm-fing' pearls because a comedian used a crude word while speaking the truth to power, but no one says shit about the swift and down-low chipping away of a woman's right to choose.

Kevin Rooney
December 30, 2017

I wonder what made Trump think he belonged in the Oval Office? Did he catch a glimpse of himself, naked in a mirror, and say, "Wow, I AM an oval, I'd fit right into the Oval Office like an organ into a slot in Operation!"

Rick Overton
July 31, 2018 • Twitter

Trump is going to start drilling for oil off the coast of Stephen Miller.

Sarah Silverman
June 22, 2018

Trump sucks (big oil's dick) and (tickles their balls).

Merrill Markoe
June 22, 2018 • Twitter

If you were an agent trying to cast a character described as "the human equivalent of an antibiotic resistant bacteria," Stephen Miller would definitely be at the top of your list.

Steve Tupper
June 6, 2018

I wonder why the Philadelphia Eagles can't show respect to the military like the President does: ripping Gold Star parents, telling a war widow her husband knew what he signed up for, openly mocking John McCain being tortured as a POW...

Larry Amoros
August 27, 2018 • 8:25 PM

Here's a question a reporter should ask Trump: "Didn't your mother teach you any manners?"

Dennis Blair
June 21, 2018

She had to wear the "I Don't Care" coat to hide the "I'm with Stupid" shirt underneath.

Rudy Reber
June 21, 2018 • Twitter

I'll be more hopeful about Melania's visit to the Texas border once I'm convinced she's not looking for some new White House gardeners.

Kevin Rooney
June 22, 2018

If what you think can be written in paint on your jacket, you need to rethink what you think.

Sarah Silverman
June 1, 2018

WE LIVE IN FUCKING INSANITY.

"Meeting the Pope"
Jonathan Schmock

Sarah Silverman
June 28, 2018 • Twitter

Our Democracy is being murdered by frauds wearing American flag pins. HAVE A GREAT THURSDAY!!

Merrill Markoe
August 18, 2018

Even though he has produced a lineage of half-wits, has a gold plated toilet and shares a lot of the behaviors of one of the lesser remembered Roman emperors, Trump is not a king.

Larry Amoros
June 23, 2018

Today Sarah Sanders was denied service at Big Huck's Feed Barn and Slop House.

Rob Becker
June 24, 2018

Trumpers finally speaking out about the inhumane atrocity - at the Red Hen. #empathy

Leah Krinsky
June 25, 2018 • Twitter

Hey, Sarah Sanders: don't think of it as being asked to leave a restaurant, think of it as being forcibly separated from your entrée. #FamiliesBelongTogether

Mike Rowe
June 25, 2018

What people aren't reporting about the Red Hen is that Sarah Huckabee wasn't wearing shoes and a shirt.

Rob Becker
June 24, 2018

A Trump supporter lecturing about civility is like O.J. offering couples counseling.

Jason Stuart
2018

As her platform, Melania Trump wants to stop bullies. I say start by rolling over in bed, taking the pillow and putting it over your husband's mouth.

Leah Krinsky
June 12, 2018 • Twitter

Maybe some good will come of this, like Trump emulating Kim Jong Un's practice of killing off family members. #TrumpKimSummit

Merrill Markoe
June 12, 2018

And by "great personality" Trump means, "Didn't contradict anything I said, told me I looked thinner and handsomer in person, and asked to see a brochure about membership in Mar-a-Lago."
#KimJongUn

Dennis Blair
June 13, 2018

"Kim Jong Un loves his people." Yeah, the way Kathy Bates' character loved James Caan's character in "Misery."

Larry Amoros
July 28, 2018

DONALD TRUMP IS STAGING A KOOK DÉTAT.

"Meeting

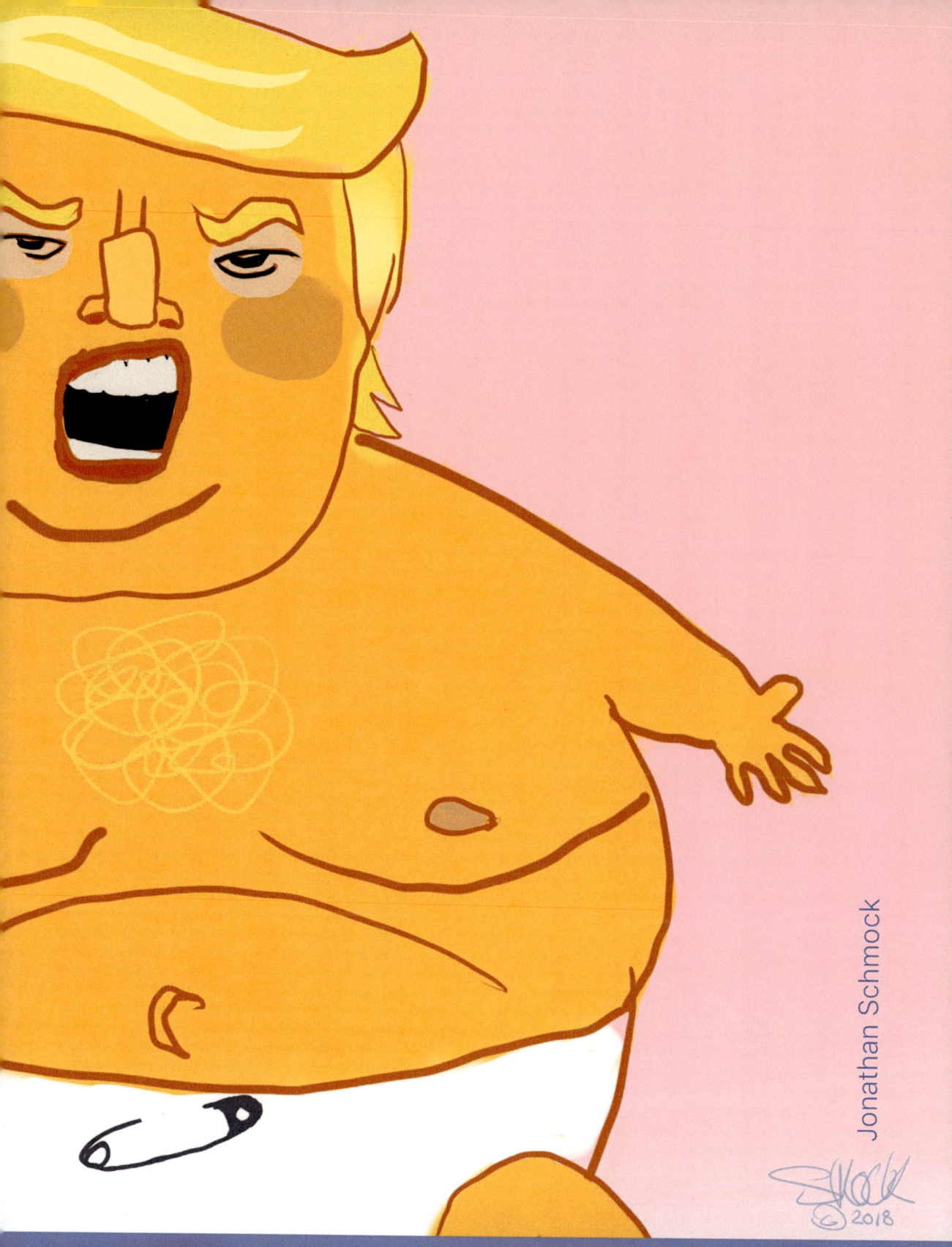

the Queen"

Mike Rowe
July 13, 2018 at 12:54 PM

I'm watching the protesters in London. Trump finally got the crowd size he wanted.

Carl Reiner
July 18, 2018 • Twitter

Nobody is more perceptive than President Trump. On seeing a blimp flying over London depicting him as an overweight baby, he understood and reacted quickly by saying, "I feel unwelcome."

Rob Becker
July 18, 2018

"I stand for the anthem, but I kneel before Putin."
　　　　　　　　　　　　 – every phony GOP "Patriot"

Kevin Rooney
July 24, 2018

"What you're seeing and what you're reading is not what's happening." – Trump to his base.

If you are a Republican, it is time to pick up after your dog.

"Helsinki"
Jonathan Schmock

John DeBellis
July 30, 2018 • Twitter

The Democrats have proof that Trump has been sucking up to Russia. They found Putin's DNA on his nose.

Rob Becker
August 7, 2018 at 4:19 PM

Cut Trump some slack. This is the first time he's run a big country while being blackmailed by the Russian Mob.

Kevin Rooney
July 8, 2018

Trump with Putin is like the dumb businessman who believes the lap dancer who tells him that he's different from the others and that she "really, really" likes him. Putin got Trump's last single, and all Trump got was some side-tit.

Merrill Markoe
August 27, 2018

Trump says he misspoke on Russia meddling following Putin meeting. Or, as Richard Pryor liked to put it, "Who are you going to believe? Me or your lying eyes?"

Rob Becker
2018

The News should just be called, "Let's See What Trump is Lying About Today".

Kevin Rooney
July 26, 2018 at 10:19 PM

Uh-Oh. My advice to Michael Cohen, in Russian: "Serpentine, Michael, serpentine!"

Sarah Silverman
June 3, 2018

White people who aren't aware of the massive amounts of racism and inequality in this country are like pretty girls who think "Everyone's so nice!"

Sarah Silverman
June 2018

Dear Members of ICE: "Just following orders" is what Nazis said during the Nuremberg trials. It is YOU who are doing these things. YOU are ripping children from their parents & holding them in cages. History will see that you carried out these crimes against humanity. YOU.

Sarah Silverman
June 2018

I'm gonna hold these children hostage until Dems agree to all the shitty things I want = This is on the Dems. You're a damaged man. You're emotionally able to ruin these children's lives & use them as pawns because your life was ruined as a child. PLEASE GET HELP.

Sarah Silverman
July 2018

I get it, @GOP - I know that even those among you with consciences are too scared to speak out. There's no middle ground. It's like finding a wallet: either you return it and you're a hero, or you keep it & are a shithead. Only it's not a wallet, it's people.

Larry Amoros
June 23, 2018

Ronald Reagan called his wife "Mommy."
George Bush married his mommy.
Dubya needed his mommy.
Pence calls his wife "Mother."
Trump is a motherfucker.
Republican men have issues.

Leah Krinsky
June 29, 2018 • Twitter

Trump is reportedly considering two women for the Supreme Court. So fingers crossed, Barbi Twins! #SCOTUS

Sarah Silverman
2018

I really try to be positive, but he truly is the most colossal shit-scented douche bag of all time.

Mark Brazill
2018

Great, now even the little countries will know how stupid we are. #TrumpAtTheUN

Steve Tupper
June 6, 2018

Aaaah, yes. How could I forget the passage in the Bible where Jesus told his disciples to draw a line in the dirt and separate mothers from their children if they crossed it? I believe it was called "The Parable of Human Infestation."

John DeBellis
June 30, 2018

Trump wants to close the borders to keep the rapists out. He doesn't like the competition.

Carol Siskind
2018

My hair was straight before this shit show.

William Stephenson
September 26, 2017

The problem is not that Puerto Rico sits in the middle of the ocean. It's the 3 ½ million Puerto Ricans sitting on the island. #resist

Carl Reiner
2018 • Twitter

To learn who Trump truly is, unscramble the word with the following letters: C-A-R-S-I-T.

Mark Brazill
2018

Remember when he said, "Whataya got to lose?" Now you know.

Larry Amoros
2018

Today, Trump announced he's starting a "Space Force". Can't wait til next week when he's gonna be a cowboy, and then a superhero, a baseball player and a ballerina.

Larry Amoros
2018

Trump's original name for his Space Force was "Super Duper Sky Fighters" - but it was too long to fit on a hat.

Rick Overton
2018

We can't even escape to Mars, now. The Space Force is already there and charging New York rental rates.

Larry Amoros
2018

How great would it be if, when Trump's Space Force lands on Mars, they find that all the people there are Mexican?

Rob Becker
September 26, 2017

An Uber driver told my daughter that the weather is being controlled from outer space – by Democrats.

Neal Brennan
Twitter

For a phony Witch Hunt, there sure are a lot of brooms and pointed hats and cauldrons.

Rob Becker
2018

You never forget that first indictment.

Mike Dugan
2018

Trump has so many skeletons in his closet, there's barely room for Pence.

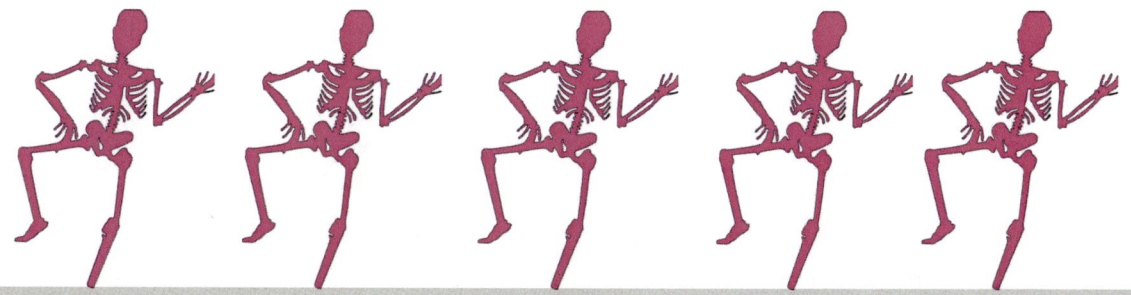

Larry Amoros
May 12, 2017

Sarah Huckabee Sanders: Christian liar. Nice.

William Stephenson
May 2, 2018

When you tell the truth, you don't worry about setups or traps or people flipping on you.

Jonathan Schmock

John DeBellis
2018

You can count how many times Trump really reached out to minorities on his middle finger.

Sarah Silverman
2018

UR racist arrogant garbage, and history will remember U that way & I know U asked Jeff Ross if my tits were real (they are). Now pack 4 HELL, Mary.

Mark Brazill
June 19, 2018

Sessions says it's a different policy; "Hitler kept the Jews in." He SAID this.
#Racist #DeportionCamps

Sarah Silverman
2018

Donald Trump is fake news. The pathology is that literally anything he accuses others of is what he himself is doing.

"Mueller!!!!!!!!!!!!!!!!!!!"

Carl Reiner
2018 • Twitter

After successfully firing members of the FBI and his White House staff, Trump asked his son and son-in-law to look into the possibility of deporting any citizens who voted for Hillary.

Sarah Silverman
2018

Senator Cruz, I'm dying to know: do you earnestly believe that these men are protesting the National Anthem?

Rob Becker
July 17, 2018

Hey, Trump, I'd stand for the Anthem, but I have bone spurs.

Rob Becker
July 27, 2018

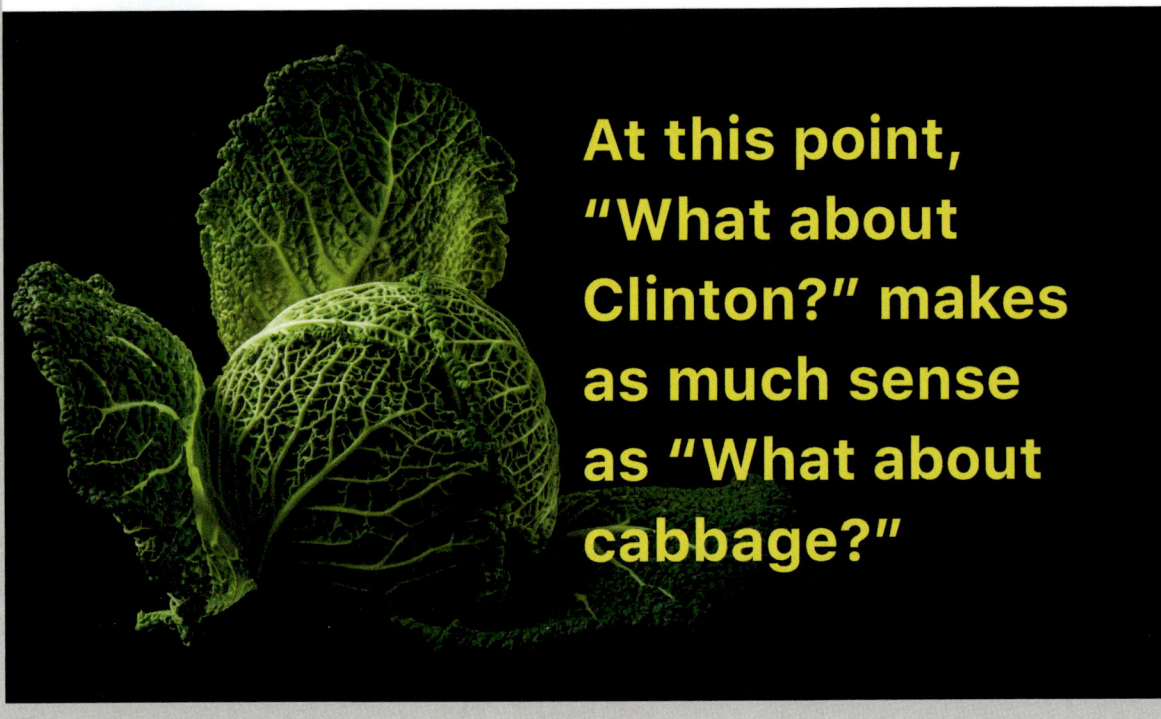

At this point, "What about Clinton?" makes as much sense as "What about cabbage?"

Rob Becker
2018

@RealDonaldTrump I seriously think Hillary needs a restraining order. Move on, Dude.

Dana Gould
2018

How many weeks away are we from Rudy Giuliani going on TV just to fart in a kid's pool and shout at the bubbles?

Kevin Nealon
2018

The Tooth is the Tooth Giuliani

Carl Reiner
July 25, 2018 • Twitter

The nooooooooooooooooosssssssssssssssse is tightennnnnnnnnniiinnnnnnngggggg.

William Stephenson
July 25, 2018

This Trump thing is such a slow burn. When it's done, the meat will just fall off the bone.

Rob Becker
August 29, 2018

Trump is a trapped rat, clawing at the lid on Pandora's box.

Sarah Silverman
August 2018

The difference between humans and animals used to be that humans possess reason. Now the difference is that animals have an instinct to take care of abandoned babies that are not their own, and humans do not.

Rob Becker
June 20, 2018

I hope the Trumps aren't separated when they go to prison. #Families BelongTogether

Larry Amoros
August 22, 2018

When Jared Kushner gets indicted, do you think they'll read the indictment from right to left?

Kevin Rooney
2017

Not only was Trump's inauguration crowd less than half the size of Obama's, his memorial will be too. And most of them will only be there to make sure he's dead.

Kevin Rooney
August 29, 2018 at 1:04 PM

Trump heart attack Kit: Wall-to-wall coverage of glowing tributes to John McCain, Obama speaking, and Hillary sitting in the front row. Even on FOX.

Kevin Rooney
August 2018

When Trump dies, he will put the "fun" in funeral.

Dana Gould
August 29, 2018

The President is jealous of the attention paid to John McCain's death.

He does not seem to mind that over 500 immigrant children still sleep in cages because of his cruelty and incompetence.

It makes you wish that Hell was real.

Bill McCarty
July 16, 2018

Anyone who still supports Traitor 45 should just admit that they neither love nor understand America.

Merrill Markoe
2018

If you are supporting this administration, you are out of your mind.

"Soiling"

Jonathan Schmock

Made in the USA
Lexington, KY
01 December 2018